Try This, It Might H
Poetry and Verse

Published by Parks & Mews 2023

ISBN:9781739113339

Other poetry collections
from Catherine West-McGrath:

Homesick for the North and Other Poetry

Lapsed Capitalist: A Poetry Collection

Optimistic Activist: Poetry and Verse

British Values: A Poetry Collection

What She Really Means and Other Poetry

The Poems and Lyrics

*Lyrics

Try This, It Might Help

One person
Listens
They hear
Their feelings
Their moments
Told through
Your words

One person
Begins to see
Their story
Is not unique
Their treatment
Was not
Unusual

One person
Understands
They are
Connected
To you if only
Through a shared
Experience

One person
Opens the window
The breeze of a new day
Brushing their face
Because of you
They know
They are not alone

The Reporter

She gathered stories
Found traces made links
Drew pictures
Released words in bits

Edited headlines
Neat introductions
Summaries
Enticed readers

Her own hidden
Under newsprint in a corner
Lifted one day
To find a lost shoe

There it was
Hers alone
Discoloured paper
Folded in her old diary

I'm Not Dancing

Just because I know these steps
Doesn't mean I have to dance
I used to move so easily
When you gave me the chance

I watched myself from deep within
Follow your rhythmic beat
Your confidence ensured our bond
Our coupling complete

I learned the steps in younger days
Not knowing there was more
But now I know quite differently
Know what my feet are for

This dance floor doesn't hold the same
Appeal as once it might
I'll use my wings to soar instead
Now watch as I take flight

Victim Blaming

See the lines and grids created
Tracks the flows of comms restated
Solid perfect watertight
Trained to know it's always right
Sure this system always will
Protect those who believe and still
For others who may feel its harms
Who cry for help or raise alarms

These single ones have failed its test
Unlike ourselves who try our best
We wouldn't make their one mistake
Their own bad choice was theirs to make
Faith so strong can't be rejected
Believe it keeps us well protected
Let victims be rebuked and shamed
The system must be always tamed

I See You

I go out in the rain
To take photographs
Of all of the clouds
And umbrellas

I go out in the dawn
When nobody's out
Only the newsboys
And homeless fellas

I take pictures of walls
And littered doorways
Where people have slept
In detritus

I pick up empty cups
And forgotten dreams
To tidy away
Another night of

I met you on the street
In front of those gates
Beside the entrance
To the station

I See You cont.

I knew just who you were
You don't need to say
We both know the chords
Our complication

Ahhhhh
Ahhhhh

You see me and
I see you
We both share so much history
We know we know we know
You see me and
I see you
But nobody sees you in
Nobody sees you in
Nobody sees you in me

No nobody sees you in
Nobody sees you in
Nobody sees you in me

The Alternative Four Es

Today we're boosting Empathy
No more we will reject
Instead you'll see an upward tick
In caring and respect

Now we move to Equality
The scales balanced at last
Injustice based on wealth and birth
Confined now to the past

Next let's see our Environment
Repaired and loved once more
Let no one harm the Earth for gain
Instead we must restore

The last E is for Everyone
Greed for the few unfair
It's true no justice can be done
Until our wealth is shared

Keep Remembering

I heard about you and I'm coming to regret
The ones I listened to who told me to forget
I was persuaded we had nothing left to say
Forgot those struggles and the fights of yesterday
But now I'm tracing back to find my history
To understand events that shape my family
Why were the stories told that hoped we would divide?
Who hoped our freedoms would be weakened and denied?

We're never gonna break our ties again
We're singing for the women and the men
Those gone before us and the ones who still remain
We're never gonna break our ties again
Together we will keep remembering

I found your letters and the banners that you made
Among the diaries and the posters on display
You stood on lines and fought for every victory
I didn't realise the things you did for me
So now I'm learning of the fights you fought and won
And of the fights for justice only just begun
Even today we know those struggles still go on
But in our unity we'll take on anyone

Not Growing

I'm not growing today
I've decided to rest
There's a reason for seasons
Nature always knows best

I'm resisting the podcasts
And the books on the shelf
With the message that growth
Makes a happier self

I'll switch off, take a break
From the gurus of change
Who insist that I must
See my life rearranged

Springtime needs Winter too
Needs a time to be slow
There's a reason for seasons
So for now I won't grow

Power of Poetry

Haven't time to write a thesis
Print a book to share my views
I've no agent making phone calls
Making sure I make the news

I'm no film star winning Oscars
Who can make a speech on stage
Bringing focus to an issue
That has made this actor rage

So instead I'm writing poems
Some are short but nonetheless
These illuminate emotions
On each feeling I confess

Through the craft of words and language
I'm connecting rhythmically
With the poet in each person
That's the power of poetry

Steel

Feel feel through the steel
Too easy to be numb
But the crying's real
Sigh, cry, one more try
Oh
Feel feel
Is there a human heart
Under the steel, steel
And can we ever start
To open up the cage
To let it heal?

That day at the river
We could see so clear
Don't you remember?
Didn't I say?
You are needed here?
That day when you called me
I ran straight back to you
Don't you remember?
Didn't I say?
You will make it through?

That day you were so sad
I wiped away your tears
Don't you remember?
Didn't I say?
You'll find your happy years?
That day you were leaving
I said the future's bright
Don't you remember?
Didn't I say?
Everything's alright?

Stained Glass Picture Window

The stained glass picture window
That makes us
Oh oh
x 2

I turn the telescope
From the cosmos towards me
An inward voyageur
Making a huge discovery
A scientist making the map
To guide me back to me
Illuminates my colours
In all their vibrancy

The rainbow in the patterns
Geometric in design
Within me is the beauty
Now I know is always mine
How could I think that I was dull?
I couldn't be more wrong
Inside me was the beauty
Of the stained glass all along

Zest for Life

Take some time
To measure
All the good things
All around
Then in time
You'll treasure
Every sight
And every sound
Next thing that you know
You have a

Zest for life
A zest for life
Every waking moment
For the rest of life
You can have a
Zest for life
A zest for life
Every waking moment
For the rest of your life

Take some time
To capture
Every good
That comes your way
Soon your heart's
In rapture
Hold that joy
And it can stay
Next thing that you know
You have a

Zest for Life cont.

Zest for life
A zest for life
Every waking moment
For the rest of life
You can have a
Zest for life
A zest for life
Every waking moment
For the rest of your life

Take some time
For thinking
Of the wonderous
Things you'll do
Then in time
You're blinking
As your dreams
Are coming true
Next thing that you know
You have a

Zest for life
A zest for life
Every waking moment
For the rest of life
You can have a
Zest for life
A zest for life
Every waking moment
For the rest of your life

Our Lady of Perpetual Help

She looks at us directly
Clasping her son
Safe in loving arms
Aware of his destiny

Through storms and invasions
Displacement and illness
War and neglect
Loss and need

Appearing in apparitions
To tell of her wishes
Where she should rest
In the Via Merulana

Venerated and protected
Adored and worshipped
The hope of each child
Prays a miracle will begin

Please Yourself

An exam in Spring
Passed with great effort
Next step university
A school is pleased

A wedding in Summer
White dress for the bride
To reflect the guests' hopes
A congregation is pleased

A mortgage for a new house
Full home at Christmas
Everyone is remembered
A family is pleased

A step on the ladder
New promotion to tell colleagues
Hard work is paying off
A manager is pleased

A child on the way
The Christening is arranged
Prayers and hymns welcome
A Church is pleased

A fall from running faster
Limbs have buckled
Under weighted thoughts
No one is pleased

Quadrant

Above to the Left
There's Kind to be Cruel
Fall for this little trick
You'll be branded a fool

Now this Top Right hand
Such a pleasure to find
When we meet someone who
Is just Kind to be Kind

Underneath Bottom Left
We see Cruel to be Cruel
At the edge of extreme
To avoid is the rule

Below Right obvious
We are going to find
Quite a different view
Which is Cruel to be Kind

Human Factors

Human factors
Were to blame
Mistakes to give
Another name

A list unchecked
A box unticked
A loop not closed
A stitch unpicked

A tired team
Forgot to ask
Are all of us
Up to the task?

Compassion is a Slippery Slope

Compassion is a slippery slope
Be careful if you should
Start practicing its dark arts
It must be understood

Compassion, if once taken
Can be too hard to quit
When warmth seeps in the depths of us
We can't get rid of it

Compassion's known to soften
An armour hard to touch
It's known to break and weaken
If we consume too much

Compassion's not forgotten
. Once tasted will connect
The parts of us left broken
From hatred and neglect

Return to the Abbey

I sneaked in through a back door
Sat in a pew at the back
Of the empty chapel
Bathed in light from above
Remembering love

Letters came frequently
Postcards too
Long passages
Instilling reassurance
Whenever you need me

No matter what happens
No matter where our paths
Take us no matter
You have a friend in me
Be confident in that

As I was leaving, quietly
I noticed his robes first
We crossed on the corridor
His cold stare piercing
I didn't belong in his palace

That's Enough

Okay okay you've had your play
Come back to me but yesterday
I said you could, out of the blue
Have some time off, time just for you

I gave you space to take a break
Control over the choice you'd make
Find time to read or learn a skill
Or find a few short hours to kill

Could share a coffee in the week
With someone who might let you speak
Where you'd become with every word
A person newly being heard

So you could feel a little more
As your old self, like you before
You turned your thoughts to pleasing me
Which I accepted willingly

No Apology

Can I hold him just once
Now you'll kiss him Goodbye
She walked out of the room
I was hearing you cry
You'll get over it soon
It's for best that you leave
Forget all these nine months
And, remember, don't grieve

Leave your shame in the past
Single mums don't belong
In the nursery rooms
You've been judged to be wrong
We can both rinse our hands
As we take him away
This is not the state's fault
There's no sorry to say

You Can Go Home Now

We observed you
From a safe distance
As the vehicle spun
In flames
Careful to see
You weren't fully
Extinguished

Your bones are crushed
And broken
Don't look in the mirror
Your face is unrecognisable
Red and blue
From bruises, cuts
And swelling

But the car has
Come to a stop now
Its wheels have gone but
The steering is still
Connected although
The windscreen is cracked
Discharged without advice

You can go home now

Coming Home

Hey how you doing?
I know it's been too long
And now I stand before you
To admit that I was wrong
To let you feel abandoned
I never meant you ill
I know I was mistaken
But you'll forgive me still

Coming home coming home
I'm not alone not alone
Where have I been
For all these years?
Spent too much time
In fear
I'm coming home coming home
I'm not alone not alone
Now I have the choice
I'm coming home

Hey do you remember?
The day I closed the door
Believed if you were hidden
I believed I'd hurt no more
Denied that you were part of me
I tried hard to ignore
Even the days I heard your voice
Those days I heard you roar

Hey, about us two
Make time we could be friends?
I know that you've been hurting
And I want to make amends
I realise the only way
For you and I to heal
Is if I stop denying
And admit the pain was real

Only the Beer is for Sale

The man, after ordering his pint
Turned to his pal and mumbled
Yet I heard him swearing
In between words like
Her
Warm
Bed
Tonight

As I placed the glass on the towel
I missed and the beer was thrown
Towards his trousers
As the glass exploded I
Could
Only
Look
Away

Kindness Seeds

Take your packet
Of kindness seeds
At the beginning
Of the day
Hold them
In your hands
Press them
To your heart

As your day continues
Your kindness seeds
Will need nurturing

Kindness seeds need
The soil of connection
The water of compassion
The warmth of love
The light of hope
Patience to develop and
Gentleness to flourish

If you wish
Your kindness seeds
To thrive
Keep them out
Of environments
In which
They might be harmed

Alcocer, Guanajuato

Each day we eat with a new family
Thin soup and cabbage
We are special guests
Today there is chicken

Breakfast is beans and coffee
We rise at dawn to help
Make fresh tortillas
To eat in the day

Later we go to the tienda
Buying cakes and Coca Cola
Poured into bags with straws
The children shout 'Hola' as they pass

We build toilets in adobe cabins
In the evening watch soap operas
Adverts interrupt to sell things
Our families can't afford

We are guests at a wedding
The priest comes from miles away
Everyone stands
Goats wander in to spectate

We dance at the wedding feast
The young couple smile
I take photos to send back
To Alcocer, Guanajuato

Holy Saturday

The in-between day
The darkest day
The waiting day
The saddest day

Yesterday the shock
Seemed immense
Today we are suffering
The hours feel too long

Despite our pleas
The hurt settles
The loss envelopes us
The pain stings

Innocent victims
Crushed by injustice
Whatever words we use
Always misunderstood

We never planned
To be travelling
Through No-man's Land
With no map or destination

We think we are alone
But we are never alone
We think we are unloved
But we are never unloved

The dawn will come
The hope will come
New light will come
New life will come

Baby Girl

Baby girl
Baby girl
It's late and morning's near
Late and morning's near
Baby girl
Baby girl
Your mummy and daddy are here
Mummy and daddy are here

And we'll rock you sound to sleep
Pray the angels gonna keep
Watch over you
In the morning we can play
And we'll play and play all day
Promise you
Made a wish and you came true

Baby girl
Baby girl
It's dark but have no fear
Dark but have no fear
Baby girl
Baby girl
No monsters to come near
Monsters to come near

Let us sing you songs of love
While the moon and stars above
Shine the whole night through
And tomorrow in the sun
We'll go out and have some fun
Promise you
Made a wish and you came true
You came true

Baby girl
Baby girl
Baby girl
Baby girl

Fix the System Not the Person

Encouraged to comply
No chance to ask 'why?'
Or protest if we see something's wrong
If we question at all
Sometimes wonder if
We'll ever belong
Then
We learn it's not us
We were not the wrong fit

Relieved
At last we can breathe
Life's no longer a test
We were always enough
Now we know
We can start to
Fix the system
Not the person

Compliance Defiance Alliance

Certainly
Of course
My
Pleasure
Lovely
I'm
Always
Nice
Caring
Every time

Deluded
Enemies
Frenemies
I'm
Angry
No-one
Cares
Exhausted

Aware
Listening
Liking
I'm
Attempting
Nuance
Compassionately
Evolving

Isolated Incident

This was a one-off
You were unlucky
Unfortunate
Perhaps by your
Own mistakes. Don't

Make a fuss
No need to
Rock the boat
They're under
Pressure. Perhaps

Best to remove
Yourself
Remembering
Won't do you
Any good. Until

Someone else
Tells of a similar
Event from
Another time
Another place. But

Isolated Incident cont.

Your thoughts
Their words
Slowly unfolding
Your fears
Soothed. Now

The alone
Becomes the
Reunited
Survivors finding
Each other. Stories

Connecting our
Shared memories
Perhaps this
Wasn't an
Isolated incident
After all

Flame

A weak purple flame
Low by the wick
One breath away
From a cold empty stick
Discovered in time
Before it was gone
Heard a thought in a heart
Saying, 'I can't go on'

So the candle, protected
Left its cold windowsill
To be carried through streets
To be sheltered until
It could find a new home
Where its flame would grow bright
Unaware of the fires
That its sparks would ignite

Climbing Mountains

As a child you held my hand
I would run alongside
As you taught me
How to climb mountains

Today I held your hand
As you climbed your last
No words were needed
After all the conversations

When you reached the summit
We let go, you were safe
Because of you I was safe
To go on, climbing mountains

I'm Listening

When no one close
Wants to listen
Distractions
Are too satisfying
To resist

Or there isn't
The bandwidth available
To allow you
The space
To feel heard

When attempts
To connect
Are met with silence
Or sometimes
Even rage

There will always
Be someone
Who comes along
Who will say
'I'm listening'

English Summer

When the English Summer
Comes around again
We will walk by yellow churches
And pretend
We were never ever lovers
Only gave ourselves to others
Watching sunsets
Wishing these days never end

In the meadow
By the tall grass
And you pointed to the hill
Said,'We'll climb it'
In the evening
Watch the swallows
Long until
Picking daisies
Finding poppies
Scent of jasmine in the air
Dragonflies upon the water
Brought a picnic
We could share

Bells were pealing
From the steeple
So we had to take a look
Found a choir
On the altar
Singing from a holy book
Climbed the tower
Of the cathedral
Saw the city down below
If you'd asked
I would have said, 'Yes'
But instead
We'll never know

A New Chapter

I've been stuck on this page
In a paragraph repeating
The dialogue
My monologue
Resonates in the print against
The cream

Some characters I've given
Too much significance
Imagining they are
Central to my story
Captivated by their subplot
Forgetting I'm the author

I've imagined the page so heavy
Now it's almost weightless
I have no option
But to see what's next
How wonderful a new chapter
Is just a page turn away

Count Every Good Word

For every 'no thanks'
Count every 'thanks so much'
You'll have far far more

For every 'not this time'
Count every 'of course'
You'll have far far more

For every 'unfortunately'
Count every 'congratulations'
You'll have far far more

For every 'you're not invited'
Count every 'please come along'
You'll have far far more

For every 'you're too much'
Count every 'you're just right'
You'll have far far more

For every 'don't be stupid'
Count every 'brilliant idea'
You'll have far far more

For every 'you're not enough'
Count every 'you're amazing'
You'll have far far more

We Were Always Going to Forgive Each Other

We knew
We were always
Going to
Forgive each other

It just took
Sometime
To quiet
Our minds

To slow
Our breath
To rest
Our anger

To heal
Our hurt
To forgive
Ourselves

To remove
Our shame
To lift
Our smiles

To extend
Our hand
To take
The first step

We knew
We were always
Going to
Forgive each other

Fall in Love

Fall in

Love

With yourself

It's only by

Loving ourselves

That we can begin

To empathise

With others

And empathise

With ourselves

New Mountain Range

Sometimes the mountain we are on
Shakes and rumbles
We stumble tumble
Slipping on muddy rocks

Bruised now cut by branches
We land at the river bank
Clothes ripped
Boots scuffed

Behind us the shaken mountain
Before us a new range
Hidden previously
A new mountain to explore

Every Morning We Are Farmers

Every morning we are farmers
Checking saplings
Of dreams to come
Planted in rich soil

By day we nurture
Encouragement ensuring sunlight
Action ensuring water
At night we dream again

When cold and frost threaten
We protect
Covering in compassion
These are precious dreams

In fields we labour
At markets we trade
Returning home knowing dreams
Grow in our care

Flowers burst open to joy
Ripe fruit picked to share
Harvests announce feasting
We celebrate under canopies